A BEGINNER'S GUIDE TO CREATING PEACE AND HARMONY IN YOUR RELATIONSHIPS

WRITTEN BY MEADOWLARK MOON

COPYRIGHT AND DISCLAIMER POLICY

TABLE OF CONTENTS

We love our partners, parents, children, friends and co-workers, extended family members and neighbors. Some days there is peace and harmony at home, and we feel safe in our home sanctuary from the stressors of the outside world.

But then some days…

Some days there can be ongoing struggles and the total opposite of peace and harmony in our homes, marriages, places of work and communities.

We may be engaging in horrible verbal battles with our partner, children or parents.

We may have endless arguments with no positive resolution and we can't seem to make progress even though we argue and try.

There often seems to be a disconnect between our heart's desire for peace in the home and our actual frequent non-peaceful experiences in relationships.

Maybe you have explored the possibility of therapy for yourself or couple's therapy but your partner isn't interested.

Maybe you have looked into family therapy but the cost just creates another problem.

You might think that you need to have years of therapy to explore childhood trauma or uncover unconscious behavior patterns so that you can improve relationships.

While these approaches can be highly beneficial, I want to challenge this myth.

The three simple steps that you can learn here in just a few days and begin putting into practice can help you and your family learn to achieve the peace and harmony in your home that you long to experience and create for your family.

Over many years of intense work in Family Therapy and Crisis Counseling, I have seen relationships so full of love suffer serious pain from heartbreaking interactions because people simply do not know HOW to be in a healthy relationship.

It's easy to get stuck in negative behavioral patterns, often passed down through our parents and their parents and grandparents before them.

Little children learn relationship behaviors from families, churches, communities and cultures. Our parents, teachers and communities didn't know how to teach us healthy relationship skills so we have all been doing the best we can.

We are often taught to ignore the cues that our boundaries have been violated. We stifle the physical signs like sudden muscle tension, increased heart rate or a drop in energy in our chest areas. We might feel a churning in our belly or we might notice that our hands tighten. Maybe we suddenly find it difficult to even move or think. There can be many physical signs but we learned as little ones that social acceptance is more important. We are taught to NOT honor our personal boundaries.

In my own life, I have struggled with unhealthy relationship patterns. My first marriage was unhealthy and ended in a long and messy divorce. I have struggled with periods of estrangement from my adult children and siblings. I have experienced failed friendships. But now that I have learned healthy relationship skills, I'm able to navigate conflict and tough times in relationships in a healthy way. My home and family life are, more often than not, a place of peace and harmony. I now enjoy more close, honest relationships with family, friends, co-workers and many beautiful acquaintances.

The need for basic relationship skills became clear to me as I worked with clients and families who were struggling with the same relationship problems that challenged me.

Here are the three basic steps to enjoying healthy relationships. We will move through the steps carefully and intentionally one, at a time. There will be specific instructions for you to follow and it is important that you take time to move through the steps carefully by giving them your full attention and by following the instructions as presented here.

If you rush through the steps and begin too quickly the results will likely not improve your relationships and may even increase distress in your relationships. It is not in your best interest to rush this process.

This step-by-step process will require time and mindful self-exploration. It is entirely up to you to use this process carefully. Peace and harmony in your home begin with you.

> *"Boundaries do not mean putting up walls. It means showing others where the door is and asking them to knock".*
>
> *Ara Wiseman*

Personal boundaries in relationships are like a fence in a backyard. The fence marks and holds an acceptable area for children, pets, neighbors and others; we can let others in or out of the fenced area.

In relationships, personal boundaries are the invisible fences that we set with others. People sometimes arrive at adulthood with a fairly good sense of acceptable physical boundaries. But often, we are not even conscious of the concept that there are also emotional, mental, social and other boundaries that need to be honored.

Our families, communities, schools and churches influence our early learning and we become socialized to have unhealthy boundaries. We may have been taught to ignore the cues that our boundaries have been violated, cues such as tightness in our chest, neck and shoulders or a sudden rush or drop of energy in our bodies. We will talk ourselves into ignoring these cues so that we fit in to our families and communities.

Boundaries can be healthy or unhealthy. This is an area that needs self-exploration. Imagine a Boundary Style Continuum as illustrated below. The green center is the area where you enjoy healthy personal boundaries. To the far left, in the orange area, are very loose boundaries and to the far right, in the red area, are very tight boundaries.

Boundary Style Continuum

Loose	Healthy	Tight

The goal is to seek that beautiful point of balance, in the green area, to have healthy personal boundaries with others. How?

This first step is critical and we must understand the basic concepts. People with healthy boundaries have a balanced mixture of self-respect and respect for others. They know their own personal needs in relationships and they can respectfully maintain those needs in relationships with others. They honor their own life values and they also honor the values of others. People with healthy boundaries can accept other's personal boundaries, and they negotiate and compromise in relationships with others.

On the left extreme of the continuum, people with loose boundaries struggle with the concept of self-respect. They have trouble saying no to others even when they feel uncomfortable. They will often allow others to be disrespectful or even to abuse them.

People with loose boundaries have an open sense of where they begin and end, they don't know what they believe, or they may depend on others to form opinions for them and make decisions for them. They may tell a stranger many personal details and trust strangers too quickly for safety. They may also take on other's problems and feel responsible for other's emotions.

On the other extreme end of the above personal boundary line are tight personal boundaries. People with tight boundaries will often avoid being close to others. They don't share information and may seem aloof and distant in relationships.

They have difficulty building trusting relationships with others. They keep others at a distance both physically and emotionally. They never give themselves the chance to build healthy relationships.

YOUR WORK: Spend some time exploring your own boundaries. Which area of the Boundary Style Continuum describes you best? Just notice and don't judge anything. Notice and jot down your insights in the space below.

____

____

____

____

____

BOUNDARY CATEGORIES

Now that these basic concepts of healthy boundaries are more familiar, the next phase of developing healthy personal boundaries is to understand personal boundaries in relationships with others. To help with this understanding, we can group personal boundaries into seven categories. These seven different categories of personal boundaries are: physical, emotional, mental, time, sexual, social and ownership.

Physical boundaries refer to our personal space in the material world. Who do you want to touch your body? Some people enjoy hugging others and some people don't want to hug anyone at any time. There are often cultural expectations related to different occasions.

For instance, at a family gathering you may feel comfortable hugging everyone, but at a work gathering you may only want to shake hands with others. If I sit on a sofa next to a close family member, I feel comfortable being very close physically. But if I sit next to a co-worker, I want to be farther away physically.

Physical boundaries are violated when others touch your body without your permission. For example, when I was a child, it was considered very important to show respect to elders. This is indeed a noble idea.

However, due to subtle cultural cues and parental and Sunday School teacher guidance, I violated my own physical boundaries when I allowed elderly men to hug me even though I actually disliked even the idea.

I ignored my own physical boundaries to be socially acceptable in my community. This community pressure also taught me and socialized me to dismiss my personal boundaries. This did not serve me well as a teen and young adult as I sought to develop relationships with potential partners.

Emotional boundaries are about our feelings. A basic human need is to be heard and understood in relationships with others. Emotional boundaries can be crossed when others mock our feelings or invalidate our feelings. Also, we may violate other's emotional boundaries when we take on emotional responsibility for other's feelings.

For example, a person may understand that they need to end a relationship that is not healthy, but they choose to dishonor their own needs because they feel responsible for the other's feelings and behavioral responses.

This is a violation of emotional boundaries because we have no business there, other's emotions are their own. Caring is appropriate but taking personal responsibility crosses healthy boundary lines.

Mental boundaries refer to our opinions, beliefs, ideas and thoughts. In healthy boundaries, our own and also other's ideas and beliefs are honored and respected. As with emotional boundaries, mental boundaries are crossed when others belittle, dismiss or invalidate our ideas, opinions and beliefs. We may also violate other's mental boundaries by pushing them to think or believe the same way we think.

For example, in the last few presidential elections, even close family members would cross boundaries and push others to embrace their political thoughts and opinions. Again, each person has a right to their own thoughts and viewpoints, and it is inappropriate for those boundaries to be dishonored.

Time boundaries are related to how we choose to spend our time. Conflict can arise when we don't honor our own and other's time boundaries. Time boundaries can be violated when others insist upon taking our time for themselves.

This issue may arise at work when we are asked to stay late or work extra days unfairly. Partners, parents, friends, children and neighbors may demand time of others. We can cross boundaries in our intimate partner relationships when we demand that our partners spend a certain amount of their time catering to our needs.

Sexual boundaries. This is a tricky and complicated boundary area. Sexual boundaries are a complex mix of the other personal boundary categories including physical, time, emotional, mental, our possessions and social boundaries. In sexual relationships, healthy boundaries must include mutual respect in all of the other boundary categories.

In intimate partnerships we must work out many of these boundary areas with our partners in our own unique ways based upon each individual's personal boundaries. This is the category where we must know ourselves and our partners and honor our own and our partner's boundaries in all of these categories. Sexual boundaries can be violated outside of sexual relationships as well.

Lewd or sexual comments and behaviors, unwanted touch or pressure to engage in sexual behaviors are ways that sexual boundaries can be crossed. A violent and extreme, but not uncommon example, would be rape.

Social boundaries refer to our unique ideas about public and social behavioral expectations. For example, some couples are comfortable mingling at social gatherings separate from their mates but other couples may prefer to stay together as they mingle at parties.

Behavioral expectations in social situations can be influenced by cultural, religious, community or family rules and expectations. Adolescents especially need to be prepared to honor their personal values and personal boundaries around alcohol, drugs and sexual behaviors that arise in social situations.

Boundaries of ownership relate to the things that we own and our money. We must set limits with others on what we will share and with whom we will share. Ownership boundaries can be violated when others steal from us or damage our possessions.

Boundaries related to ownership can also be crossed when others pressure us for the use of our money or our things. I have a dear friend who often pushed me to loan my car and my boundary is that I do not loan my car to others. This relationship was so important to me that I had to honestly negotiate and compromise to keep the relationship intact.

In the above information on personal boundaries are the basic concepts for beginning to understand and set our own personal boundaries. Now, it's time to self-explore.

YOUR WORK: Using the worksheet below, explore your unique boundaries in each category and identify areas of concern in your relationships with others. For now, don't judge or critique, simply identify areas of concern. For example, at work you may be dissatisfied about the amount of overtime you are asked to take. Or there may be social boundaries that cause stress in your relationship with your partner.

You may recognize areas where you violate other's boundaries, or you may notice areas where your own boundaries are being dishonored. For now, just identify areas of concern. This takes careful thought and consideration and you must not rush the self-exploration process. Take your time and use the worksheet below as a guide.

Boundaries Worksheet

Explore your unique personal boundaries in each category.
For now, just observe and identify areas of concern in your relationships with others.
Jot down your insights on this worksheet.

Physical Boundaries

For example: John Doe hugs me at work and I don't want to be hugged.

____
____
____
____
____
____

Emotional Boundaries

For example: I feel guilty when I say no to the teacher when she wants me to lead the room parent's meeting. Or John Doe ignores me when I tell him I feel sad.

____
____
____
____
____
____

Mental Boundaries

For example: At Thanksgiving everyone tried to make me agree with them about politics. They would not listen to my opinion.

____
____
____
____
____
____

Time Boundaries
For example: The boss asks me to work late more than she asks anyone else when she knows I have to pick up the kids.

____

____

____

____

____

Sexual Boundaries
For example: At work I feel uncomfortable in the front office because my co-workers make sexual jokes and comments.

____

____

____

____

____

Ownership Boundaries
For example: Jane Doe asks to borrow money every week and she even asks to borrow my car and I don't want to loan her money or my car.

____

____

____

____

____

Social Boundaries
For example: I don't want to drink at the party but people talk me in to drinking too much.

____

____

____

____

____

STEP TWO: IDENTIFY HEALTHY COMMUNICATION STYLES

Now that you have explored your own unique boundaries in the seven categories, we can move to step 2.

We can understand the concepts related to healthy communication styles by applying a framework of respect. Let's use another continuum to illustrate communication styles.

As we saw earlier in the work with personal boundaries, we want to strive to be in the green, healthy center of the continuum. Healthy communications reflect equal respect for others and self-respect. How do we arrive at this center of balance?

Again, we must first understand the concepts of different communication styles. As you did in the work above, visualize a continuum where balance is achieved in communication style.

Boundary Style Continuum

Passive	Assertive	Aggressive
No self-respect, Only respect for others	*Balanced respect for self and others*	*Only self-respect, no respect for others*

While there are several methods to communicate with others including verbal, written and body language, there are only three main styles of communication. These communication styles include passive, aggressive and assertive styles. There is also a negative and complicated style which combines passive and aggressive styles of communication. Let's look at each style to increase understanding of the concepts.

ASSERTIVE COMMUNICATION STYLE

Assertive communicators fall in the balanced center of the continuum. Assertive communicators display an equal balance of self-respect and respect for others in relationships. They have a calm, confident presence and make appropriate eye contact with others.

They will listen to others without interrupting and will honor other's needs and boundaries in relationships. Assertive communicators can express their own personal boundaries and relationship needs and they are willing to use negotiation and compromise to achieve balance in relationships.

PASSIVE COMMUNICATION STYLE

On the left end of the line above is the passive communicator. People who use this communication style are often quiet and meek in relationships with others. They seem to be uncomfortable making eye contact with others and they do not easily express their ideas, opinions or needs in relationships. Non-verbal communication can also include a hunched over posture and very quiet vocal tone. They have an overall meek appearance and behaviors. They will allow others to lead them and will arrange themselves to meet other's needs with no honor for their own needs. Passive communicators have a limited sense of self-power and rely on others for opinions and decisions. Passive communicators may also be related to loose healthy boundaries and they have little respect for themselves.

AGGRESSIVE COMMUNICATION STYLE

On the opposite end of the communication style continuum above are aggressive communicators. These are the bullies we may have encountered in school or at work, and sometimes in our own families. Aggressive communicators have little respect for others and demand that others respect their needs, opinions and feelings.

Aggressive communicators will criticize, belittle and interrupt others, and are often easily angered. They will then speak in loud and threatening tones, display intense eye contact and may stand too close in an effort to intimidate others. Aggressive communicators may deliberately damage other's property, punch holes in walls or throw items in acts of aggression and intimidation. Aggressive communicators may also escalate to physical violence by pushing or hitting others. Aggressive communicators often expect and even demand that others take responsibility for their feelings and behavior choices.

PASSIVE/AGGRESSIVE COMMUNICATION STYLE

Mentioned earlier in this discussion were the combined styles of passive and aggressive communication. It is common in relationships for people to demonstrate passive/aggressiveness. An example of this would be when a typically passive person becomes angry and will then exhibit aggression.

Not knowing how to be assertive and respect themselves, they may slam doors loudly, curse and scream at others which is not their typical communication style. Or, they may withhold affections without expressing their feelings of anger in healthy ways.

YOUR WORK: Identify your primary style of communication and list that on the worksheet below: Assertive, Passive, Aggressive, or Passive/Aggressive. Then explore your closest relationships: partner, parents, children, siblings, friends, supervisor, co-workers and so forth and jot down their communication styles.

Using the worksheet below, think back and list some past communications in your life that demonstrate each of the communication styles. This is not for you to judge others or yourself. This work is only to self explore, observe and learn.

At this point we have completed step two which is to understand healthy communication styles and behaviors. Now, as a way to deepen your understanding, begin to pay attention to interactions in your family, your place of work, at church or other social settings.

You will begin to become more adept at recognizing healthy behaviors when you observe them as well as unhealthy interactions. This will help as you learn to achieve balance in your own interactions with others. Spend a day or two in this observation phase before moving on to step three. If you like, make note of your observations and insights using the worksheet below.

Communication Styles Worksheet

Observe areas of your life and identify areas of concern.

My main communication style is:

____

____

____

____

Partner

For example: We will yell sometimes and sometimes we will not speak- yelling is aggressive and not speaking to each other is passive.

____

____

____

____

____

Work

For example: The receptionist won't tell people that they can't smoke in the building and that's passive.

____

____

____

____

____

Church

For example: I told the Committee chair I would do that talk but I don't want to and that's passive.

____

____

____

____

____

Parenting

For example: I get aggressive when the kids ignore me so I yell and slam the door.

____

____

____

____

____

Explore other areas of life or just observe human interactions at the mall or a concert and make a note of what you noticed.

STEP THREE: PRACTICE BOUNDARY SETTING AND HEALTHY COMMUNICATION SKILLS

"Let's build bridges, not walls."

Martin Luther King, Jr

Change can be challenging. The concepts and skills that you are learning in this workbook are new and different. Please be gentle with yourself and your loved ones as you learn and practice this new information. It takes time for the brain to learn. Be aware that as YOU change and become healthier and begin setting and maintaining personal boundaries, your RELATIONSHIPS will also change.

If you are in any abusive relationships do not begin there and especially don't try these healthier skills when you're alone with aggressive communicators.

Aggressive communicators may find it difficult to change their style from aggressive to assertive quickly, just as passive communicators cannot be expected to suddenly be capable of assertive communication.

As your relationships shift into a healthier balance, you may experience a sense of unbalance in your relationships with others. You may become anxious as you begin to practice these new skills and notice that you feel shaky or your heart rate increases along with increased muscle tension. Be gentle with yourself and others as you practice. It is OK to tell those you are in communication with that you need a break for a few minutes. Be gentle with yourself and others during this learning phase. The reward for your efforts will be a gradual shift into more frequent harmony in relationships.

It would be wise for you to find support through a local counseling agency as you build these skills and examine your relationships.

A mental health counselor can help you to explore underlying relationship issues that might arise as you shift to healthier interactions. Ask your counselor to help you to create plans to keep yourself and your family safe if you are in relationship with aggressive people.

Assertive communication is a learned skill. In most of our families, we learned a mix of healthy, aggressive, passive or passive/aggressive communications. Now that you have gained an understanding of the basic concepts of personal boundaries and communication styles, it's time to learn the skills necessary to achieve balance between healthy and unhealthy boundaries as well as between passive and aggressive communications.

By using assertive communication skills, we can set and maintain healthy personal boundaries with others. There are many methods of learning assertive communication styles and a bibliography is included at the end of this workbook so that you can explore deeper concepts and assertive communication skills. For our work here, we will use a communication tool called an 'I Statement'.

There are many ways to use this tool and you can find it taught with four steps, five steps or only two steps.

Here we will use just three steps.

Step 1: I feel____.

Step 2: When____.

Step 3: I would like____.

This is a simple, but not necessarily easy, process! This 'I statement' can be used in two distinct ways. It can be used as a self-exploration tool only, or it can be used to self-explore and then plan for and implement healthy communications in relationships.

Here is an example of an important time in my life when I used the 'I statement' tool to self-explore and to communicate in a stressful work situation.

At work during a large, all staff meeting, an announcement was made about a change that directly affected me and my workload.

Having not been alerted to this change before the large meeting, I was shocked! I felt a sudden rush of physical sensations, thoughts and feelings that was confusing and difficult to manage in the moment. I handled the situation acceptably in the awkward moment, but I was left with unsettled, negative feelings and reactions.

So, over the next couple of days, I pondered the situation and my reactions by using the three step 'I statement' as a tool to simply self-explore. Having been overwhelmed with that rush, I needed to calmly consider: How did I feel? What happened to create this emotional response? What would have been better for me in that particular situation?

At this point in the process of seeking healthy balance, I just used the 'I statement' as a tool to figure out my feelings and desires in my work relationships. Here is what I came up with after taking a piece of paper and working with the tool. Remember, I did not express this yet to any co-worker. I simply used the 'I statement' formula as a self-exploration tool.

First of all, I felt surprised. This was the initial signal that a boundary violation had occurred. My body responded by increasing muscle tension, especially in my chest, neck, shoulders and face. My heart began to beat faster. I began to have worried thoughts that my salary could be negatively affected and I wouldn't be able to pay my bills.

I kept exploring.

I also felt angry. By searching a little deeper and moving underneath the anger, I discovered that I felt disrespected that I had not been included in the discussion before the announcement was made in an all-staff meeting and that I would have preferred to be informed of the change before it was announced in the large meeting.

Only then was I ready to use the tool to communicate assertively. So, I asked for a meeting with my supervisor and prepared my 'I statement,' which was "I felt surprised, angry and disrespected when it was announced in the company staff meeting that this change had been implemented. In the future, I would like to be informed of any changes that directly affect me before a companywide announce-ment."

My supervisor welcomed the meeting and after I shared the above 'I statement,' she immediately apologized, took responsibility for the oversight and promised to be more careful in the future. The result was that our working relationship strengthened. I trusted her to listen and work in a healthy way with me, and she trusted me to be honest and work in a healthy way with her. When I shared my emotions with her, it worked to help us feel more connected to each other rather than more separat-ed.

I had other behavior choices.

I could have been passive and not spoken my truth. This would likely have led to a quiet but strong resentment which would have negatively affected my relationship with my supervisor. It would most likely have negatively affected my job satisfaction. This passive decision would likely also have led to my supervisor and me feeling disconnected from each other and unsupported.

Or, I could have stood up in the meeting and chosen an aggressive outburst in that moment or even approached leadership team members after the meeting with aggressive and blaming communication which would certainly have negatively affected our working relationships and may also have even led to a disciplinary hearing or write up in my human resources file. This behavior choice would likely have led to feelings of disconnection.

This example illustrates the fact that when we use the 'I statement' to self-explore and then communicate our feelings appropriately, we take responsibility for our feelings and our needs in relationships with no blame to the other party.

We simply stand in our own truth. Then, the response is in their hands and we let go. When we can honestly express our feelings and relationship needs, we can then let go of expectations and allow others to own their feelings and behavioral responses.

In healthy relationships, this type of healthy communication can lead to negotiation and compromise. We can support our loved ones and co-workers with their own unique growth and development and we can also feel supported in our own journey. Sharing emotions using non-blaming 'I statements' help us to feel closer to others.

Now it's time for you to use the following worksheet to self-explore yourself and to practice creating 'I statements' to express your unique personal boundaries.

I Statement

Step 1. I feel____.

Step 2. When____.

Step 3. I would like____.

Examples:

I feel hurt and lonely when I tell you I'd like to spend more time with you one on one but we never do. I would like to feel close to you and that I am important to you.

I feel scared and shaky and unable to think when the yelling starts. I would like for us to take a break when we start yelling and talk about it when we are both calm.

I feel disappointed, scared and mad when we have agreed not to spend money but then another package shows up. I would like to talk about our budget again and come to a solid agreement that we can stick to together.

When we share our feelings with others it helps us to feel closer to each other. Use the worksheet to explore your own feelings and then prepare your 'I statements' for sharing with others.

Step 1. I feel____.

Step 2. When____.

Step 3. I would like____.

Step 1. I feel____.

Step 2. When____.

Step 3. I would like____.

Step 1. I feel____.

Step 2. When____.

Step 3. I would like____.

Step 1. I feel____.

Step 2. When____.

Step 3. I would like____.

Step 1. I feel____.

Step 2. When____.

Step 3. I would like____.

Step 1. I feel____.

Step 2. When____.

Step 3. I would like____.

Step 1. I feel____.

Step 2. When____.

Step 3. I would like____.

MOVING FORWARD

Congratulations! You have now completed this three-step fundamental workbook and can begin to practice putting these concepts to use in everyday relationship interactions at home, work, friendships and in all areas of life.

Be kind to yourself and to your family members as you learn these new skills.

Just as with any learning experience there will be mistakes and awkwardness. For those of us who were socialized as children to be passive, using an 'I statement' can feel scary! For those of us who have aggressive communication tendencies, it can also feel awkward and scary to practice new ways of communicating.

Sometimes, when you set healthy boundaries with others, you might get an unhealthy response from others. For example, in my work illustration above, what if my supervisor had not taken responsibility?

You may find that people in your life have negative reactions to boundary settings and healthy communication.

If this happens, there are some important steps to take.
1. Stay calm. Take a break.
2. Seek some additional support. A mental health counselor can be a helpful resource during this time.
3. Determine if the relationship is worth the effort to try again.

For those of us who learned as children to be aggressive or passive/aggressive we will need time to challenge how we were taught and to learn to be respectful of ourselves and others. Those of us who learned to be passive need time for self-worth and self-confidence to build as we practice these skills.

Always begin practicing your skills with safe people in safe situations. The more you practice, the easier this new way of interacting with others will become. Take it slow and easy and don't expect relation-ships to heal overnight or to reach perfection.

Read some books, watch some practice videos and practice your new understanding and skills often.

There is no perfection with human interaction, relationships are complex and are not static, changes happen. But when you use these skills, model these concepts and skills for others and teach these skills to your children, you will see positive changes and experience more harmonious homes, work environments and communities.

It has been my honor and privilege to be a part of your work to create happier, healthier relationships. Many blessings on your journey!
Meadowlark Moon

ADDITIONAL RESOURCES TO EXPAND YOUR KNOWLEDGE AND SKILLS

When I Say No, I Feel Guilty by Manuel Smith: This book is a well-loved classic and is written in an easy-going and fun manner. Smith explains psychological reasons for some behaviors and teaches several practical skills to help manage life situations assertively. This is my all-time favorite and has helped me navigate some challenging relationships.

Boundaries: When to Say Yes, How to Say No by Henry Cloud and John Townsend: Cloud and Townsend have written several books and workbooks to help teach people about healthy boundaries from a Christian, Biblical viewpoint. Any of their books or videos will be helpful for those who may have been taught by their religion that being passive or even violent is Biblical. They have written books for parents, spouses and more.

Your Perfect Right, A Guide to Assertive Behavior by Robert Alberti and Michael Emmons: Alberti and Emmons published their original book in the 70s and it quickly became a best seller. In recent years it has been revised and is still full of wisdom and guidance for understanding and learning to set healthy boundaries in relationships.

www.TherapistAid.com This website has many free resources on different topics including boundaries and communication skills. You can access worksheets, videos, articles and more.

Some of the information in this e-book was adapted from all of the above resources and from the author's life experiences and education. In addition to these classics above, you can find articles, podcasts, videos and blogs related to setting healthy boundaries and assertiveness training online.

Make a lifelong study of understanding and learning to set healthy boundaries in relationships!

The result can be that your life and the lives of your children and families will move forward positively and with more peace and harmony.

Disclaimer

If you are in an abusive relationship with an aggressive person, DO NOT attempt to use assertive communication skills alone. Please seek a therapist who can support your new understanding and guide you through managing unhealthy relationships.